Angelina's
Birthday Bike

Based on the original classic Angelina stories
written by Katharine Holabird, illustrated by Helen Craig
Adapted by Catherine Baker

Angelina went for a ride on her green bike.

"This is fun!" she said.

The bike hit a rock.

Angelina fell off.

"This is not fun!"
she said.

4

Angelina was sad.

"Look at my bike," she said.
"I can not ride it now."

Soon it was Angelina's birthday.

"This is fun," she said.

Angelina got a big red bike!

"I can ride my red bike!" she said.

Angelina went for a
ride on her red bike.

11

"It is fun to ride my red bike,"
said Angelina.